Dame **Shirley** Veronica **Bassey**, DBE, bo
Bute St., Tiger Bay (Butetown), Cardiff,
whose career began in the mid-1950s, b
powerful voice and for recording the theme songs to the James Bond films Goldfinger (1964), Diamonds Are Forever (1971), and Moonraker (1979). Bassey became the first Welsh person to have a No. 1 single, during January 1959.

Shirley received the Brit Award for Best British Female Solo Artist over the previous 25 years during 1977. She was made a CBE during 1994, before being created a Dame, for services to the performing arts by Queen Elizabeth II, during the year 2000. Bassey has been called "one of the most popular female vocalists in Britain during the last half of the 20th century."

Shirley was the 6th and youngest child of Henry Bassey and Eliza Jane Start, having grown up in the community of Splott, Cardiff, Wales, UK. Her father was Nigerian, and her mother was English, from Teesside in the northeast of England. Two of her mother's 4 children from previous relationships lived in the Bassey household.

Shirley's mother listed her first husband, Alfred Metcalfe, as her own father in the registry of her marriage to Henry Bassey, leading to speculation that the marriage was bigamous in the absence of a prior divorce. Eliza and Henry's second child died in infancy, so Shirley was born into a household of three sisters, two half-sisters, and one brother.

Teachers and schoolchildren at Moorland Road School noticed Bassey's strong voice, but didn't encourage her, Shirley saying: "...everyone told me to shut up. Even in the school choir the teacher kept telling me to back off till I was singing in the corridor!" A classmate remembered her singing the refrain "Can't Help Lovin' Dat Man" from Show Boat, with such feeling that she made their teacher feel uncomfortable. After leaving Splott Secondary Modern School aged 14, Bassey got a job at the Curran Steels factory, while singing in public houses and clubs during the evenings and at weekends.

During a 1999 interview with Nigel Havers in her Monte Carlo apartment, Shirley pointed to a sheet of paper framed on the wall, saying it was her first contract, with a salary of £14 a week, a considerable sum for a 16-year-old during 1953. However, upon closer inspection of the document, dated 17th December 1953, it appeared to be £10 for two performances.

That year Bassey signed a contract to sing in the touring variety show, Memories of Jolson, a musical based on the life of Al Jolson, before appearing in Hot from Harlem, which ran until 1954. However, she became pregnant at 16 with her first child, refusing to reveal the name of the child's father, returning to waitressing in Cardiff.

Shirley toured various theatres during 1955, until she was noticed by the impresario Jack Hylton, who invited her to appear in Al Read's 'Such Is Life' at the Adelphi Theatre in London's West End. Philips record producer Johnny Franz spotted her on TV during the show's run, being impressed, offering her a recording deal.

Bassey recorded her first single, "Burn My Candle", released during February 1956, when she was 19. The BBC banned it because of the suggestive lyrics but it still sold well, backed with her powerful rendition of "Stormy Weather". More singles followed before during February 1957, Shirley had her first hit with "The Banana Boat Song", which reached No. 8 on the UK Singles Chart. She also recorded under the direction of American producer Mitch Miller in New York for the Columbia label that year, issuing the single "If I Had a Needle and Thread" b/w "Tonight My Heart She Is Crying". Bassey then made her American stage début in Las Vegas, at El Rancho Vegas.

She recorded two singles during mid-1958 that became classics, "As I Love You" being released as the B-side of another ballad, "Hands Across the Sea", which didn't sell well at first, but after an appearance at the London Palladium sales began to pick up. "As I Love You" topped the UK charts during January 1959, remaining there for 4 weeks, the first No. 1 single by a Welsh artist. Bassey's recording of "Kiss Me, Honey Honey, Kiss Me," climbed the charts alongside "As I Love You", with both singles occupying the Top 3 at the same time. Shirley signed to EMI's Columbia label a few months later, beginning the second phase of her recording career.

Bassey had many hit singles in the UK, and 5 albums in the Top 15 during the early to mid-1960s. Her recording of "As Long As He Needs Me" from Lionel Bart's Oliver! reached No. 2 during 1960, having had a chart run of 30 weeks. Shirley made her American TV début on 13th November 1960, when she performed on The Ed Sullivan Show.

Her album Let's Face the Music (1962), on which she collaborated with Nelson Riddle and his orchestra, reached No. 12 in the UK, with the single, "What Now My Love" hitting No. 5. Bassey's other UK Top 10 singles included her second chart-topper, the double A-side "Reach for the Stars"/"Climb Ev'ry Mountain" and "I'll Get By" during 1961, followed by a cover version of the Ben E. King hit "I (Who Have Nothing)" in 1963.

Shirley appeared on the cover of Ebony magazine that year, having sung at a Washington gala celebrating President Kennedy's second year in office.

Bassey had her only US Top 40 Billboard Hot 100 hit single during January 1965, with the title song of the James Bond film, Goldfinger, which reached No. 8, while the original soundtrack of Goldfinger topped the US charts that year. Shirley also sang the title song for the James Bond spoof The Liquidator during 1965 then had a Top 20 live album, recorded during a sold-out run at the Pigalle in London.

Bassey recorded "Mr Kiss Kiss Bang Bang" for the next Bond film, Thunderball (1965) but it wasn't used in the movie, although the film's score followed its melodic theme. Written by John Barry and Leslie Bricusse, it was re-recorded by Dionne Warwick, after Shirley's version, before being rejected in favour of a new song, "Thunderball," hastily written by Barry, being given to Tom Jones, after the movie's producers decided the song over the opening credits had to include the film's title.

However, the "Goldfinger" theme song had a lasting impact on her career. Peter Clayton observed in the sleeve notes for Bassey's 25th Anniversary Album (1978) that: "Acceptance in America was considerably helped by the enormous popularity of "Goldfinger"...but she'd actually established herself there as early as 1961, in cabaret in New York. She was also a success in Las Vegas...'I suppose I should feel hurt that I've never been really big in America on record since "Goldfinger"...but, concertwise, I always sell out.'..."

Shirley had only one solo LP which reached the Top 20 of a US chart, R&B, Live at Carnegie Hall, so she was really a one-hit wonder. Following "Goldfinger" her UK sales started to slip as well, with only two of her singles entering the UK Top 40 from 1966 - 1970. She'd signed to United Artists, her first album on that label, I've Got a Song for You (1966), spending just one week on the chart. Between 1966 -1970, only two of her albums charted, one of those being a compilation. One of her best-known singles, "Big Spender" was issued during 1967, just missing the UK Top 20.

Bassey began to live as a tax exile in 1968, so was unable to work in Britain for almost two years. At the Sanremo Festival in Italy that year, she performed "La vita", an Italian song by Bruno Canfora and Antonio Amurri, with some lyrics having been re-written in English by Norman Newell for her. Shirley's version of the song, with its chorus sung in Italian, became a Top 40 hit in Italy, Bassey recording several other songs in Italian, some appearing on the album La vita (1968), but her UK sales continued to decline. Newell later wrote English lyrics for the rest of "La vita", producing "This Is My Life".

Shirley's UK comeback began during 1970, leading to one of the most successful periods of her career, having started the decade with a BBC TV 'Special' The Young Generation Meet Shirley Bassey, recorded in Sweden, shown on BBC1 on 18th March. She returned to the UK with a record-breaking run of performances at the Talk of the Town nightclub.

That year her L.P. 'Something' (UK # 5), was released, showcasing the new Bassey style, shifting from traditional pop to more contemporary songs and arrangements. The title track single was more successful in the UK charts than the original recording by The Beatles, hitting # 4, also being a Top 10 US hit on the Adult Contemporary chart. However, she never completely abandoned what that had been her forte: standards, show tunes, and torch songs.

Shirley's singles of the period included the hit "Never Never Never", an English version of the Italian "Grande grande grande", which reached the Top 10 of the US Adult Contemporary Chart, the UK Top 10 and No. 1 in Australia and South Africa. Returning to the James Bond franchise, she recorded the theme song for Diamonds Are Forever during 1971.

The success of "Something" led to a series of successful albums on the United Artists label, including Something Else (1971), And I Love You So (1972), I Capricorn (1972), Never Never Never (1973), Good, Bad but Beautiful (1975), Love, Life and Feelings (1976), You Take My Heart Away (1977) and Yesterdays (1978).

Two of Bassey's earlier LPs also entered the charts during the '70s: And We Were Lovers (1967, re-issued as Big Spender), and Let's Face the Music (1962, re-issued as What Now My Love). Two compilations, The Shirley Bassey Singles Album (1975) and the 25th Anniversary Album (1978), both made the UK Top 3: The Shirley Bassey Singles Album, her highest-charting LP, hit No. 2, being certified gold, while the 25th Anniversary Album eventually went platinum.

Shirley had 18 L.Ps in the UK Albums Chart between 1970 and 1979, with her L.P. The Magic Is You (1978) having featured a portrait by the photographer Francesco Scavullo. Her sold-out concerts at New York's Carnegie Hall were recorded and released as a two-LP set during 1973, Shirley Bassey: Live at Carnegie Hall. This album and the majority of her recordings from this period were later issued on CD by EMI and BGO Records.

Bassey was twice the subject of This Is Your Life, first during November 1972, when she was surprised by Eamonn Andrews at Heathrow Airport then during January 1993, when Michael Aspel surprised her at the curtain call of a sell-out concert at the Royal Albert Hall. Shirley appeared on the Morecambe and Wise Christmas Show, broadcast on Christmas Day of 1971.

Bassey starred in the 6-episode The Shirley Bassey Show during 1976, the first of her TV programmes for the BBC, followed by a second series of 6 episodes during 1979. The final show of the first series was nominated for the Golden Rose of Montreux during 1977. The series featured guests including Neil Diamond, Michel Legrand, The Three Degrees and Dusty Springfield, with Shirley appearing at various international locations as well as in the TV studio. Bassey pled guilty to being drunk and disorderly during 1978 "after shouting abuse in the street and pushing a policeman". She closed out the decade with her third title theme for a Bond film, Moonraker (1979).

For most of the 1980s, Shirley focused on charitable work and performing occasional concert tours throughout Europe, Australia, and the United States. She'd ended her contract with United Artists, whose former record division had become part of EMI, having begun what she said was her "semi-retirement". Bassey recorded the L.P. All by Myself during 1982 then made a TV special for Thames Television called A Special Lady, with guest Robert Goulet.

Shirley recorded a duet with the French film actor Alain Delon, "Thought I'd Ring You" during 1983, which became a hit single in Europe. Although she was recording far less frequently, an album of her most famous songs, I Am What I Am (1984), was recorded with the London Symphony Orchestra (LSO) conducted by Carl Davis. Bassey played the Friday night at Henley Festival during 1984.

This was followed by a single and video to support the London Tourist Board, "There's No Place Like London" (1986), which was co-written by Lynsey de Paul and Gerard Kenny. Shirley recorded a L.P. of James Bond themes, The Bond Collection during 1987, but wasn't happy with the results so decided not to release it, but 5 years later it was issued anyway, so Bassey sued in court, with all unsold copies being withdrawn.

Shirley then provided vocals for Swiss artists Yello on "The Rhythm Divine" (1987), a song co-written by Scottish singer Billy Mackenzie, before an album sung entirely in Spanish, La Mujer was released during 1989. Bassey had started working with a vocal coach, during the mid-1980s, who was a former opera singer, with several songs on her L.P. Keep the Music Playing (1991), being in a grand, operatic pop style, perhaps also having been influenced by her album with the LSO 7 years earlier.

EMI issued the 5-CD box set Bassey – The EMI/UA Years 1959–1979 during 1994, with an accompanying booklet, opening with a poem by Marc Almond. Shirley collaborated with Chris Rea in the film La Passione (1996), appearing in the movie as herself then releasing the single "'Disco' La Passione", with the remix of the single charting just outside the UK top 40.

Bassey's "History Repeating", written for her by the Propellerheads, reached No. 1 on the UK Dance Chart, and No. 10 on the US Dance Chart during 1997, also having been a Top 10 hit in Italy. The liner notes of the Propellerheads' album Decksandrumsandrockandroll included the lines: "We would like to extend our maximum respect to Shirley Bassey for honouring us with her performance. We are still in shock...."

Shirley celebrated her 60th birthday that year with two open-air concerts, at Castle Howard and Althorp Park, and another TV special. The resulting live L.P., The Birthday Concert, received a Grammy Award nomination for Best Traditional Pop Vocal Performance. Bassey performed for a benefit at an open-air concert close to the Sphinx and the Great Pyramid in Egypt, on 7th October 1998.

Bassey was sued in a breach of contract case that year, by her former personal assistant, who also accused Shirley of hitting her and making an ethnic slur but Bassey won the case. The case was lampooned by Alexander Baron, in his one-act play The Trial of Shirley Bassey. She performed the official song for the rugby World Cup, "World in Union", with Bryn Terfel during 1999, at the opening ceremony held in The Millennium Stadium, Cardiff, wearing a gown designed on the Welsh flag. The single made the Top 40, with Shirley contributing two more songs to the official album Land of My Fathers, which reached No. 1 on the UK compilations chart, being certified silver.

Bassey was the principal artiste at the Duke of Edinburgh's 80th birthday celebrations during 2001 then on 3rd June 2002 she was one of a prestigious line-up of artists including Elton John, Paul McCartney and Tom Jones, who performed at the Queen's Golden Jubilee Party at Buckingham Palace. Shirley celebrated 50 years in show business the following year, with the issue of the CD Thank You for the Years, which was another Top 20 album.

A gala charity auction of her stage costumes at Christie's, "Dame Shirley Bassey: 50 Years of Glittering Gowns", raised £250,000 for the Dame Shirley Bassey Scholarship at the Royal Welsh College of Music and Drama and the Noah's Ark Children's Hospital Appeal. Bassey then topped the bill at the 2005 Royal Variety Performance, introducing her new song "The Living Tree".

Two popular Audiences with Shirley Bassey have aired on British TV, one during 1995 that attracted more than 10 million viewers in the UK, with the second being broadcast during 2006. Shirley returned to perform in 5 arenas around the UK in June that year, culminating in a concert at Wembley stadium.

She also performed a concert in front of 10,000 people at the Bryn Terfel Faenol Festival in North Wales, broadcast by BBC Wales. Marks & Spencer signed her up for their Christmas 2006 James Bond-style TV ad campaign. Bassey was seen in a glamorous Ice Palace singing a cover version of Pink's song "Get the Party Started", wearing an M&S gown.

"The Living Tree", written, produced and originally recorded by the group Never the Bride, was released as a single on 23rd April 2007, marking Shirley's 50th anniversary in the UK Singles Chart – and the record for the longest span of Top 40 hits in UK chart history. Bassey performed a 45-minute set at the 2007 Glastonbury Festival, wearing a pink Julien Macdonald dress, and customised Wellington boots.

A new L.P., Get the Party Started, was issued on 25th June 2007, having entered the UK Albums Chart at No. 6, with the single of the title song hitting No. 3 on the US Dance Chart. That same year, Shirley performed "Big Spender" with Elton John at his annual White Tie and Tiara Ball, to raise money for The Elton John AIDS Foundation. Bassey also performed at Fashion Rocks, in aid of The Prince's Trust at the Royal Albert Hall, during 2007.

On 23rd May 2008 she was rushed to hospital in Monaco, to have an emergency operation on her stomach, after complaining of abdominal pains, having been forced to pull out of the Nelson Mandela 90th Birthday Tribute concert because of her illness. A biography, Diamond Diva, was published that year.

Bassey recorded the album The Performance during 2009, which reached # 20 in the UK, being certified gold, with James Bond composer David Arnold having co-produced with Mike Dixon. A number of artists wrote songs expressly for Shirley, including the Manic Street Preachers, Gary Barlow, Tom Baxter, KT Tunstall, the Pet Shop Boys, Nick Hodgson of the Kaiser Chiefs, John Barry and Don Black. Bassey headlined at the BBC Electric Proms on 23rd October 2009, her only full live set of 2009.

She performed several of the new songs from The Performance the following month on several TV shows: The Graham Norton Show, The Paul O'Grady Show and as the guest singer on Strictly Come Dancing. Shirley performed at a gala celebrating the 80th birthday of Mikhail Gorbachev on 30th March 2011 then at the Classical Brit Awards that year, singing "Goldfinger" in tribute to John Barry.

The BBC broadcast a 70-minute drama entitled Shirley on 29th September 2011, depicting Bassey's early life and career, in which Ruth Negga played the title role. Shirley was one of the line-up of artists on 4th June 2012 who performed at the Queen's 60th Jubilee Party at Buckingham Palace, singing "Diamonds Are Forever". She then performed at the Academy Awards on 24th February 2013, to commemorate the 50th anniversary of the James Bond movie franchise, her first appearance at an Oscars ceremony as a performer, having sung "Goldfinger" to a standing ovation.

Bassey performed "I'm Still Here" tuen "The Lady Is A Tramp" on 13th November 2014 at the Royal Variety Performance, in the presence of The Duke and Duchess of Cambridge. Her L.P., Hello Like Before was released on 17th November 2014, which included a 50th-anniversary re-recording of "Goldfinger", recreating the original orchestration, and a duet of "Diamonds Are a Girl's Best Friend" with Paloma Faith, produced and conducted by Stuart Barr. Bassey starred in a 60-minute BBC broadcast hosted by David Walliams during December 2016.

BBC TV Series

TV Specials

Total # Series # Title Director Original airdate

1 1 "Shirley Comes Home" Selwyn Roderick 3rd September 1957 BBC TV at 6:45pm

From the bright lights of Las Vegas and the West End, Shirley Bassey returned to her own people in the heart of Cardiff's dockland. Also at the party were: Gladys Morgan, Jimmy Rogers and 'The Black and Whites'. Introduced by Alun Williams from Cardiff's Queen Alexandra Dock.

2 1 "Shirley Sings and Riddle Swings" Yvonne Littlewood 23rd June 1962 BBC TV at 8:20pm

Shirley Bassey, Nelson Riddle and his Orchestra and The Hi-Lo's. Introduced by David Jacobs.

3 1 "International Cabaret presenting Shirley Bassey" Buddy Bregman 25 April 1964, BBC2 at 9:40pm

Starring Shirley Bassey with Robert Clary and The Ted Heath Orchestra. Musical director: Harry Rabinowitz. With The Heralds and the International Cabaret Dancers. Repeated on BBC1 18th August 1964 at 8:25pm.

4 1 "Show of the Week: The Sound of Shirley Bassey" Stewart Morris 22 February 1966, BBC2 at 8:50pm

Recorded on the eve of her departure for a world tour. Orchestra directed by Kenny Clayton.. Repeated 8 July 1967 at 7:40pm.

5 1 "The Shirley Bassey Show" Tony Charmoli 12 April 1969 BBC1 at 7:40pm

Shirley Bassey sings and introduces her guests Noel Harrison and Laurindo Almeida.

6 1 "Show of the Week: Shirley Bassey at Bern's Restaurant" Stewart Morris 6 July 1969 BBC2 at 9:55pm

Shirley Bassey at Bern's Restaurant, Stockholm. Orchestra directed by Alyn Ainsworth. A BBC co-production with Sveriges Radio. Repeated on BBC1 September 20, 1969 at 7:30pm.

7 1 "The Young Generation Meet Shirley Bassey" Stewart Morris 18 March 1970 BBC1 at 8:00pm

From the Cirkus Studio in Stockholm, Sweden. With Udo Jürgens, Andre Tahon and Ray Dondy with Alyn Ainsworth and his orchestra. A joint BBC/SR production.

8 1 "Shirley Bassey Singing Special" Stewart Morris 13 August 1970 BBC1 at 9:10pm

Tonight this international singing star makes one of her rare appearances in this country. With Brian Fahey and his orchestra. Repeated on BBC2 December 23, 1970 at 9:20pm.

9 1 "Night Club starring Shirley Bassey" John Ammonds 11 June 1972 BBC2 at 11:05pm

An international cabaret from London, introduced by Francis Matthews. Also starring Trio Athenee, Rod Hull and Emu, Alfredo Alex Welsh and his Band, Joe Castor and Partner and the Pamela Devis Dancers. The Night Club Orchestra directed by Johnny Harris.

10 1 "Show of the Week: Shirley Bassey" Dieter Finnern 28 September 1972 BBC2 at 9:25pm

Shirley Bassey on location in Sardinia and Berlin sang some of the songs which had made her famous. With the SFB Orchestra directed by Brian Fahey. A BBC/SFB Co-production.

11 1 "Shirley Bassey"Stewart Morris 26 December 1972 BBC1 at 9:55pm

Shirley Bassey, recently returned from a record-breaking appearance in New York. With 'Segment' choreographed by Nigel Lythgoe and featuring Alyn Ainsworth and his orchestra.

12 1 "Shirley Bassey at the Royal Albert Hall" Johnnie Stewart 1st January 1974 BBC1 at 9:25pm

Orchestra directed by Arthur Greenslade. Repeated on 19 April 1974 at 8:15pm.

13 1 "Shirley" Stewart Morris 28 December 1974 BBC1 at 8:30pm

Starring international singing star Shirley Bassey with her special guest Neil Diamond. Orchestra directed by Arthur Greenslade.

14 1 "Shirley Bassey"Stewart Morris 27 December 1975 BBC1 at 8:20pm

From the triumphs of a world tour, this superbly talented artist arrived for another high-flying television special. Shirley sang many of her famous hits together with a selection of new songs. Orchestra directed by Arthur Greenslade. Repeated on BBC2 April 16, 1976 at 9:10pm.

15 1 "Shirley Bassey: I Am What I Am" Mike Alexander 30 July 1994 BBC1 at 9:50pm

In a documentary that was almost as revealing as her dresses, Shirley Bassey talked about her work and the cost to her family life.

16 1 "The Shirley Bassey Concert" Gavin Taylor 30 July 1994 BBC1 at 10:40pm

Footage of a performance shot the previous September, as Shirley Bassey opened Cardiff's new International Arena with two sell-out shows before an audience of 11,000 fans.

17 1 "Shirley Bassey: This Is My Life" Alan Lewens 2 January 1998 BBC1 at 10:05pm

A documentary portrait of the internationally-acclaimed vocalist, following her travels through New York, London and Monte Carlo. The programme contained intimate moments behind the scenes, as well as capturing her performances on the stage. Repeated 7th April 2000.

18 1 "Shirley Bassey: Viva Diva!" Mike Mansfield 31 December 1998 BBC1 at 9:10pm

Shirley Bassey sang a selection of show stopping songs, with the help of a large orchestra, the cast of the hit West End stage musical Chicago and a million pounds' worth of diamonds.

19 1 "Dame Shirley Bassey: Electric Proms" Janet Fraser Cook 24 October 2009 BBC2 at 10:40pm

The singer celebrated 50 years in the business with a special performance at London's Roundhouse. Repeated multiple times on BBC HD and BBC4.

20 1 "Imagine... Dame Shirley Bassey" Dione Newton 24 November 2009 BBC1 at 10:35pm

Dame Shirley Bassey: The Girl from Tiger Bay. A profile of the Welsh singer on the release of The Performance, an album of songs composed for her by, among others: Gary Barlow, Rufus Wainwright and KT Tunstall.

Shirley Bassey (Series 1)

Produced by Stewart Morris.

Broadcast Saturdays on BBC1.

Total # Series # Title Director Original airdate

1 1 "Episode 1" Stewart Morris 30 October 1976 at 8:15pm

Making for BBC TV, the first series in her outstanding career. Guest stars: Charles Aznavour, The Three Degrees and 'Emma' (Bassey's Old English Sheep Dog). With The Shirley Bassey Dancers choreographed by Nigel Lythgoe and Arthur Greenslade and his orchestra.

2 2 "Episode 2" Stewart Morris 6 November 1976 at 8:15pm

Guest stars Rolf Harris, Janis Ian, The Brythoniad Male Voice Choir and 'Emma'. With The Shirley Bassey Dancers choreographed by Nigel Lythgoe and Arthur Greenslade and his orchestra.

3 3 "Episode 3" Stewart Morris 13 November 1976 at 8:15pm

Guest stars Johnny Nash, Gilbert O'Sullivan and 'Emma'. With The Shirley Bassey Dancers choreographed by Nigel Lythgoe and Arthur Greenslade and his orchestra.

4 4 "Episode 4" Stewart Morris 20 November 1976 at 8:15pm

Guest stars Morris Albert, The Stan Getz Quartet and 'Emma'. With The Shirley Bassey Dancers, choreographed by Nigel Lythgoe and Arthur Greenslade and his orchestra.

5 5 "Episode 5" Stewart Morris 27 November 1976 at 8:35pm

Guest stars Mel Torme, Clive Westlake and 'Emma'. With The Shirley Bassey Dancers choreographed by Nigel Lythgoe and Arthur Greenslade and his orchestra.

6 6 "Episode 6" Stewart Morris 4 December 1976 at 8:35pm

Guest stars Bobby Goldsboro, Rod McKuen and 'Emma'. With The Shirley Bassey Dancers choreographed by Nigel Lythgoe and Arthur Greenslade and his orchestra. This programme was selected as the BBC's entry for the Festival of the Golden Rose of Montreux 1977 and was repeated on BBC2 April 7, 1977 at 8:25pm.

7 7 "Highlights compilation" Stewart Morris 23 December 1977 at 9:15pm

Shirley Bassey introduces highlights from her 1976 television series. Guest stars Charles Aznavour, Rolf Harris, Johnny Nash and 'Emma'.

The series, excluding the 7th highlights episode, was repeated on BBC2 on non-consecutive Thursdays, from 23 June – 4 August 1977.

Shirley Bassey (Series 2)

Produced by Stewart Morris.

Broadcast alternate Saturdays on BBC1.

Total # Series # Title Director Original airdate

8 1 "Episode 1" Stewart Morris 30 September 1979 at 8:20pm

The first programme of a new series of 6 TV spectaculars, with her guest stars: Dana, The Three Degrees and Sal Davis. With

The Shirley Bassey Dancers, choreographed by Nigel Lythgoe and Arthur Greenslade and his orchestra.

9 2 "Episode 2" Stewart Morris 13 October 1979 at 8:15pm

Guest stars: Freddy Cole, Paul Daniels and Tony Monopoly. With The Shirley Bassey Dancers, choreographed by Nigel Lythgoe and Arthur Greenslade and his orchestra.

10 3 "Episode 3" Stewart Morris 27 October 1979 at 8:15pm

Guest stars: Lulu, The Drifters and Demis Roussos. With The Shirley Bassey Dancers, choreographed by Nigel Lythgoe and Arthur Greenslade and his orchestra[76].

11 4 "Episode 4" Stewart Morris 10 November 1979 at 8:15pm

Guest stars: Les Dawson, The Nolan Sisters and Third World. With The Shirley Bassey Dancers, choreographed by Nigel Lythgoe and Arthur Greenslade and his orchestra.

12 5 "Episode 5" Stewart Morris 24 November 1979 at 8:15pm

Guest stars: The King's Singers, Michel Legrand and Dusty Springfield. With The Shirley Bassey Dancers, choreographed by Nigel Lythgoe and Arthur Greenslade and his orchestra.

13 6 "Episode 6" Stewart Morris 8 December 1979 at 8:15pm

Guest stars: Lennie Bennett & Jerry Stevens, Pete Conrad and The Swingle Singers. With The Shirley Bassey Dancers, choreographed by Nigel Lythgoe and Arthur Greenslade and his orchestra.

Series repeated Mondays on BBC2, from 15 September – 20 October 1980 at 8:15pm.

Bassey's first marriage was to Kenneth Hume in 1961, the couple having separated during 1964 then divorced in 1965, following her affair with actor Peter Finch. Shirley then announced to the press that she and Finch would not be marrying, telling the press: "It simply wouldn't work out. Just now I'm not ready for marriage to anyone. I feel I have to be free."

A year later, Hume sued the actor and another man, John McAuliffe, for being "indiscreet" with Shirley. Both Finch and McAuliffe were cited as co-respondents in the Hume–Bassey divorce. For her part, Shirley was named as co-respondent during 1965, when Finch's wife, South African actress Yolande Turner, divorced the actor.

Sergio Novak, the assistant manager of the Excelsior Hotel in Venice, Lido, Italy, and Bassey were married from 1968 until they divorced during 1979. Novak served as Shirley's manager throughout this time. With Novak she adopted her grand-nephew, Mark.

The fathers of Shirley's two daughters, Sharon Bassey (a.k.a. Sharon Novak, 1954) and Samantha Bassey (a.k.a. Samantha Novak, born 1963), are unknown.However, Shirley's first husband suggested that Samantha, born during the couple's marriage, was the result of an affair between Bassey and Peter Finch.

During 1965, an article in Jet stated, "There is a big dispute in London over who is the father of tempestuous singer Shirley Bassey's baby. Although one-time boyfriend Australian actor Peter Finch agreed that the child may not belong to Shirley's divorced husband, Kenneth Hume, Finch insists she does not belong to him ... "

During 1985, Samantha, aged 21, was found dead in the River Avon in Bristol, England. Shirley has always maintained that the death of her daughter was not a suicide. On 24th March 2010, Avon and Somerset Police confirmed that they were carrying out fresh inquiries into the death, following claims that the convicted killer Michael Moffat was involved in her death. However, during October 2010 it was reported that the investigation had come to an end, having concluded that there "is no evidence of any criminal act involved" in Novak's death.

Bassey stated during 2009 that she and her son, Mark, had reconciled. Shirley has 4 grandsons through her surviving daughter, Sharon Novak. Bassey lives in Monaco.

Awards and achievements

"For services to entertainment", Shirley was created a Dame Commander of the Order of the British Empire (DBE) on 31st December 1999 by Queen Elizabeth II. She was invited to perform in 2002 at the Party at the Palace, a public celebration of the Queen's Golden Jubilee. She was awarded France's top honour, the Legion d'Honneur in 1999, to signify her popularity and importance to the culture of France.

During 2012, Bassey was among the British cultural icons selected by artist Sir Peter Blake to appear in a new version of his most famous artwork – the Beatles' Sgt. Pepper's Lonely Hearts Club Band album cover – to celebrate the British cultural figures of his life that he most admired. She was named as one of "the 50 greatest Welsh men and women of all time" during 2016.

1959: Favourite British Female Singer – NME Award

1972: Best Female Singer – TV Times

1973: Best Female Singer – TV Times

1974: Best Female Entertainer – American Guild of Variety Artists

1976: Best Female Singer – Music Week

1976: 22-day British tour to mark twenty years as a recording artist

1976: EMI Award for twenty years as a recording artist – UK

1977: Best British Female Solo Artist in the previous 25 years – BRIT Award

1977: Golden Rose of Montreux nomination for The Shirley Bassey Show

1991: Walk of Fame, Star Boulevard – plaque unveiled in Rotterdam

1994: CBE – Commander of the Order of the British Empire

1995: Showbusiness Personality of the Year – Variety Club of Great Britain

1997: Grammy nomination – The Birthday Concert (recorded live at Althorp Park)

1998: Longest run by a solo artist (ten shows) – Royal Festival Hall, London

1999: Légion d'Honneur – France

1999: Madam Tussaud's waxwork unveiled in London (second model in Las Vegas)

2000: DBE – Dame Commander of the Order of the British Empire

2000: Most Successful British Female Singer – Guinness Book of Records

2003: Outstanding Contribution to Music – National Music Awards, UK

2003: Lifetime Achievement Award (inaugural award) – Western Mail Welsh Woman of the Year Awards

I'm2004: "100 Great Black Britons", Bassey voted into the top ten

2004: Artist for Peace Award – UNESCO

2004: Welsh Legend Award, presented at the opening of the Cardiff Millennium Centre

2005: Avenue of Stars – plaque unveiled in London

2008: "Goldfinger" – United Artists single (1964) inducted into the Grammy Hall of Fame

2017: Hall of Fame Award, Jersey Style Awards

2017: Nordoff Robins O2 Silver Clef Award

Bibliography

"Shirley Bassey: Diamonds Are Forever" - Mary Long (2017)

Miss Shirley Bassey – John L. Williams (2010) – London: Quercus. ISBN 978-1-84724-974-6

Shirley Bassey: Diamond Diva – Peter Hogan (2008)

Cardiff: Rebirth of a Capital (Foreword by Shirley Bassey) – Ungersma, Hurn (2005)

Shirley Bassey: Welsh History Stories – Evans, Stokes, ap Emlyn, ap Emlyn (2003)

Shirley Bassey: An appreciation – Muriel Burgess (1998, reprinted 1999)

My Life on Record and in Concert – Shirley Bassey (Bloomsbury, 1998)

The Trial of Shirley Bassey – A Play in One Act – Alexander Baron (1998)

Shirley Bassey: This Is My Life (Piano/vocal/guitar) – Sheet music book

Shirley Bassey: You're the Voice (Piano/vocal/guitar) – Sheet music book

Guinness Book of British Hit Singles – 14th Edition – ISBN 0-85156-156-X

Guinness Book of British Hit Singles – 16th Edition – ISBN 0-85112-190-X

Guinness Book of British Hit Albums – 7th Edition – ISBN 0-85112-619-7

The Book of Golden Discs – 2nd Edition – ISBN 0-214-20512-6

The Guinness Book of 500 Number One Hits – ISBN 0-85112-250-7

Discography

Studio albums

Year Album title Label Peak positions UK certifications BPI

UK NLD GER US 200 US R&B

1957 Born to Sing the Blues (10" LP) Philips — — — — — —

1959 The Bewitching Miss Bassey — — — — — —

The Fabulous Shirley Bassey EMI Columbia 12 — — — — —

1961 Shirley 9 — — — — —

Shirley Bassey 14 — — — — —

1962 Let's Face the Music issued in the US as Shirley Bassey Sings The Hit Song From "Oliver!" 12 — —
— — —

1965 Shirley Stops the Shows issued in the US as Shirley Bassey Belts the Best! —— — 85 —
—

1966 I've Got a Song for You issued in the US as Shirley Means Bassey United Artists 26 — — —
— —

1967 And We Were Lovers — — — —
— —

1968 12 of Those Songs EMI Columbia 38 —
— — — —

This Is My Life United Artists — — — —
— —

This Is My Life (La vita) (Italian release) — — —
— — —

1969 Does Anybody Miss Me — — — —
— —

1970 Something issued in the US as Shirley Bassey Is Really "Something"
5 23 — 105 29 —

1971 Something Else 7 — — 123 —
—

1972 I Capricorn 13 — — 94 —
—

And I Love You So 24 — — 171 —
—

1973 Never Never Never 10 — — 60
34 Silver

1974 Nobody Does It Like Me — 32 — 142
— —

1975 Good, Bad but Beautiful 13 — — 186
54 Silver

1976 Love, Life and Feelings 13 — — 149
— Silver

1977 You Take My Heart Away 34 — —
— — —

1978 Yesterdays — — — — —
—

1979 The Magic Is You 40 10 — —
— —

1982 All by Myself issued in the UK and some other countries as Love Songs Applause 48 — —
— — —

1984 I Am What I Am Towerbell 25 — 39
— — Gold

1989 La Mujer Mercury PolyGram — —
— — — —

1991 Keep the Music Playing Later re-issued as The Power Of Love and Old Friends And Lovers FreeStyle Dino 25
— — — — —

1992 The Bond Collection Icon Records — —
— — — —

1993 Sings the Songs of Andrew Lloyd Webber EMI MFP Premier 34 — — — — —

1995 Sings the Movies issued in Germany as Showtime
PolyGram TV 24 — 94 — —
Gold

1996 The Show Must Go On PolyGram TV 47 —
— — — Silver

2000 The Remix Album...Diamonds are Forever EMI
62 — 63 — — —

2003 Thank You for the Years Sony TV Citrus 19 —
— — — Silver

2007 Get the Party Started Lock Stock and Barrel 6
— — — — Silver

2009 The Performance Geffen 20 — 81
— — Gold

2014 Hello Like Before RCA 24 — —
— —

"—" denotes releases that did not chart or were not released in that territory.

Live albums

Year Album title Label Peak positions UK certifications BPI

UK US 200 US R&B

1965 Shirley Bassey at the Pigalle issued in the US as In Person EMI Columbia 15 — — —

1970 Live at Talk of the Town United Artists 38 — — —

1973 Live at Carnegie Hall — 136 20 —

1974 Live in Japan (Japanese release) — — — —

1978 Live in Japan '77 (Japanese release) — — — —

1997 The Birthday Concert (Grammy Award nomination) Artful — — — —

Compilation albums

Year Album title UK UK certifications BPI

1968 Golden Hits of Shirley Bassey 28 —

1971 It's Magic 32 —

The Fabulous Shirley Bassey 48 —

1972 The Shirley Bassey Collection 37 —

1974 The Very Best of Shirley Bassey — Silver

1975 The Shirley Bassey Singles Album 2 Gold

The Shirley Bassey Collection Volume II — —

1976 Shirley Bassey — Silver

Thoughts of Love 15 Gold

1978 25th Anniversary Album3 Platinum

1988 Singles Album — Silver

1992 The Best of Shirley Bassey 27 —

1994 Bassey - The EMI/UA Years 1959 - 1979 — —

1995 The Best of — Silver

1996 20 of the Best — Gold

Four Decades of Song — —

2000 The Greatest Hits - This Is My Life 54 Gold

2006 The Complete EMI/Columbia Singles Collection — —

2009 Burn My Candle - The Complete Early Years 1956-58
— —

2013 Hold Me Tight — —

2015 What Now My Love: 15 Greatest Hits — —

Other notable albums

Year Album title UK UK certifications BPI

1959 Show Boat — —

1971 Big Spender (reissue of And We Were Lovers) 27
—

What Now My Love (reissue of Let's Face The Music) 17
—

1993 10,000 Voices II — —

1999 Land of My Fathers (#1 UK compilation chart) —
Silver

2002 Party at the Palace — —

Singles

Year Title Label Album Peak positions

UK US 100 US AC NLD GER ITA

1956 "Burn My Candle" b/w "Stormy Weather" Philips
The Bewitching Miss Bassey — — —
— — —

"The Wayward Wind" b/w "Born to Sing the Blues" Non Album Track — — — — — —

"After the Lights Go Down Low" b/w "If You Don't Love Me" Non Album Track — — —
— — —

1957 "The Banana Boat Song" b/w "Tra La La" The Bewitching Miss Bassey 8 — — —
— —

"If I Had a Needle and Thread" b/w "Tonight My Heart She Is Crying" Non Album Track — — — —
— —

"Fire Down Below" b/w "You, You Romeo" The Bewitching Miss Bassey 30 — — — — —

"You, You Romeo" (B-Side to "Fire Down Below") 29
— — — — —

"Puh-Leeze! Mister Brown" b/w "Take My Love, Take My Love" Non Album Track — — —
— — —

1958 "Kiss Me, Honey, Honey, Kiss Me" b/w "There's Never Been A Night" The Bewitching Miss Bassey 3
— — — — —

1959 "As I Love You" b/w "Hands Across the Sea" 1
— — — — —

"Love for Sale" b/w "Crazy Rhythm" — — —
— — —

"My Funny Valentine" b/w "How About You?" — —
— — — —

"Night and Day" b/w "The Gypsy In My Soul" — —
— — — —

"If You Love Me (Really Love Me)" b/w "Count On Me"
Columbia Non Album Track 28 —
— — — —

1960 "With These Hands" b/w "The Party's Over" Non Album Track 38 — — — — —

"The Birth of the Blues" b/w " Careless Love Blues" Philips
Born to Sing the Blues — — — —
— —

"As Long as He Needs Me" b/w "So in Love" Columbia
Non Album Track 2 — —
— — —

1961 "You'll Never Know" b/w "Hold me Tight" Non Album Track 6 — — — — —

"Reach for the Stars" b/w "Climb Ev'ry Mountain" (double A-Side) Non Album Track/Shirley Bassey 1 120
— — — —

"I'll Get By" b/w "Who Are We?" Non Album Track
10 — — — — —

1962 "Tonight" b/w "Let's Start All Over Again" Non Album Track 21 — — — — —

"Ave Maria" b/w "You'll Never Walk Alone" Non Album Track 31 — — — — —

"Far Away" b/w "My Faith" Non Album Track 24 — — — — —

"What Now My Love?" b/w "Above All Others" Let's Face the Music 5 — — — — —

1963 "What Kind of Fool am I?" b/w "Till" Non Album Track 47 — — — — —

"I (Who Have Nothing)" b/w "How Can You Tell?" Non Album Track 6 — — — — —

"Puh-Leeze! Mister Brown" b/w "The Wayward Wind" (re-release)Philips Non Album Track — — — — — —

1964 "My Special Dream" b/w "You" Columbia Non Album Track 32 — — — — —

"Gone" b/w "Your Love" Non Album Track 36 — — — — —

"Who Can I Turn To?" b/w "To Be Loved By A Man" Non Album Track — — — — — —

"Goldfinger" b/w "Strange How Love Can Be" Goldfinger OST 21 8 2 5 8 2

"Now" b/w "How Can You Believe?" Non Album Track — — — — — —

1965 "No Regrets" b/w "Seesaw Of Dreams" Non Album Track 39 — — — — —

"It's Yourself" b/w "Secrets" Non Album Track — — 38 — — —

1966 "The Liquidator" b/w "Sunshine" The Liquidator OST — — — — — —

"Don't Take the Lovers from the World" b/w "Take Away" United Artists Non Album Track — — — — — —

"Shirley" b/w "Who Could Love Me" I've Got a Song for You — — — — — —

1967 "The Impossible Dream" b/w "Do I Look Like A Fool" And We Were Lovers — — — — — —

"If You Go Away" b/w "Give Him Your Love" — — — — — —

"Big Spender" b/w "Dangerous Games" 21 — — — — —

1968 "This is My Life" b/w "Without A Word" This Is My Life — — — — — —

"La Vita (This Is My Life)" b/w "Without A Word" (Italian release) This Is My Life (La vita) — — — — — 34

"Domani, Domani" b/w "Pronto...sono io" (Italian release) — — — — — —

"To Give" b/w "Yes" (Italian release) — — —
— — —

"To Give" b/w "My Love Has Two Faces" Non Album Track
— — — — — —

"If You Go Away" (Alternative version) b/w "E'giorno" (Italian release) Non Album Track — — — —
— —

1969 "Chi Si Vuol Bene Come Noi..." b/w "Epirops" (Italian release) Non Album Track — — — —
— 18

"Does Anybody Miss Me" b/w "Fa Fa Fa (Live For Today)"
Does Anybody Miss Me — — — —
— —

"Com'è Piccolo Il Mondo" b/w "Manchi solo tu" (Italian release)
Non Album Track — — —
— — —

"Concerto D'autunno" b/w "My Way Of Life" (Italian release)
Non Album Track — — —
— — 56

"As I Love You" / "Kiss Me Honey Honey Kiss Me" (re-release)
Philips The Bewitching Miss Bassey — —
— — — —

"Fa Fa Fa (Live For Today)" b/w "The Bus that Never Comes" (German release) United Artists Non Album Track
— — — — — —

1970 "The Sea and Sand" b/w "What About Today"
Something — — — — — —

"Something" b/w "Easy To Be Hard" 4 55 6
10 40 —

"Something" b/w "Ore che sei que" (Italian release) —
— — — — —

1971 "The Fool on the Hill" b/w "What Are You Doing The Rest Of Your Life" Non Album Track 48 —
— — — —

"(Where Do I Begin?) Love Story" b/w "For The Love Of Him"
Something Else 34 — — —
— —

1972 "Diamonds are Forever" b/w "Pieces Of Dreams"
Diamonds are Forever OST 38 57
14 — — —

"Una Cascata di Diamanti (Vivo Di Diamanti)" b/w "Diamonds are Forever" (Italian release) — — — —
— —

"For All We Know" b/w "What's Done Is Done" I Capricorn
6 — — — — —

"I've Never Been a Woman Before" b/w "The Greatest Performance Of My Life" — — —
— — —

"And I Love You So" b/w "I Don't Know How To Love Him"
And I Love You So — — —
— — —

"The Ballad of the Sad Young Men" b/w "If I Should Find Love Again" — — — — — —

1973 "Jezahel" b/w "Day by Day" (German release) — — — — — —

"Never, Never, Never" b/w "Day by Day" (#67 US R&B) Never Never Never 8 48 8 13 48 —

"Make the World a Little Younger" b/w "The Old Fashioned Way" — — — — — —

1974 "When You Smile" b/w "The Trouble With Hello Is Goodbye" Nobody Does It Like Me — — — — — —

"Davy" b/w "The Trouble With Hello Is Goodbye" — — 44 — — —

"Yesterday When I Was Young" (live) b/w "Goldfinger" (live) (Japanese release) Live In Japan — — — — — —

1975 "Good, Bad, but Beautiful" b/w "I'm Nothing Without You" Good, Bad but Beautiful — — — — — —

"Living" b/w "Everything That Touches You" — — — — — —

1976 "Natali" b/w "Runaway"Love, Life and Feelings — — — — — —

"Can't Take My Eyes off You" b/w "Born To Lose" Non Album Track — — — — — —

1977 "I Let You Let Me Down Again" b/w "Razzle Dazzle"
You Take My Heart Away — —
— — — —

"You Take My Heart Away" b/w "I Let You Let Me Down Again"
— — — — — —

1979 "This is My Life (La Vita)" (re-recording) b/w "The Magic Is You" ("Copacabana (At The Copa)" (US release)) The Magic Is You — — — 5 — —

"Moonraker (Main Title)" b/w "Moonraker (End Title)"
Moonraker OST — — — —
— —

1980 "I (Who Have Nothing)" b/w "Goldfinger" (reissue)
EMI Columbia Non Album Track — —
— — — —

1982 "All By Myself" b/w "Only When I Laugh"
Applause Records All By Myself — —
— — — —

1983 "Thought I'd Ring You" (with Alain Delon) b/w "Memory" Polydor Records Non Album Track
— — — 13 — —

1984 "Remember" (with Al Corley) b/w "Thought I'd Ring You" (with Al Corley) (re-recording) Non Album Track
— — — — — —

"That's Right (Love Is No Game)" b/w "Memory" Non Album Track — — — — — —

"Sometimes" b/w "He Needs Me" Towerbell Records
Non Album Track 86 — —
— — —

"Natali" (re-recording) b/w "As I Love You" (re-recording)
I Am What I Am — — — —
— —

"I Am What I Am" b/w "This Is My Life" (re-recording) —
— — — — —

"If You Don't Understand" b/w ""To All The Men I've Loved Before" — — — — — —

1986 "To All the Men I've Loved Before" b/w "I Am What I Am" 86 — — — — —

"There's No Place Like London" b/w "Born to Sing Forever"
Non Album Track — — —
— — —

1987 "The Rhythm Divine" (Yello featuring Shirley Bassey) Mercury Records One Second 54 — —
24 47 —

1988 "Love Is No Game" b/w "Memory" Indisc Non Album Track — —— — — —

"Sin Ti" b/w "Hoy No Tengo Nada" Mercury Records
La Mujer — — — — — —

1990 "How Do You Keep the Music Playing" b/w "The Greatest Love of All" FreeStyle Keep the Music Playing
— — — — — —

1996 "He Kills Everything You Love" PolyGramTV The Show Must Go On — — — — — —

"'Disco' La Passione" (with Chris Rea) East West Records La Passione 41 — — 21 — —

1997 "History Repeating" (Propellerheads featuring Shirley Bassey) (#1 UK Dance) (#10 US Dance Club) Wall of Sound Decksandrumsandrockandroll 19 — — 52 65 8

1999 "Light My Fire" (Shirley Bassey meets Booster) Bluenote, EMI Non Album Track — — — — — —

"World in Union" (duet with Bryn Terfel) Decca Records Land of My Fathers 35 — — — — —

2000 "Where Do I Begin" (Away Team remix) Liberty, EMI The Remix Album...Diamonds are Forever 100 — — — — 51

2002 "You Can Have Him" (remix) (DJ Guy Gerber featuring Shirley Bassey) Whoop! Records Non Album Track — — — — — —

2005 "Diamonds from Sierra Leone" (Kanye West featuring [an uncredited] Shirley Bassey) Roc-A-Fella Records Late Registration 8 43 — 56 67 —

"That's What Friends Are For" (remix)	ZYX Records	Golden Disco-Hits	2	—	—	—	—	—	—

2007	"The Living Tree"	Lock Stock & Barrel	Get the Party Started	37	—	—	—	—	—

"Get the Party Started" (#3 US Dance Club)	47	—	—	—	—	—

"Big Spender" (remix)	—	—	—	—	—	—

EPs

Year	EP

1957	Shirley Bassey at the Cafe de Paris (Live recording)

1958	As I Love You

Blues by Bassey

Love for Sale

1959	The Fabulous Shirley Bassey

The Fabulous Shirley Bassey No.2

Showboat-Excerpts

Showboat-Excerpts No.2

1960	As Long as He Needs Me

1961	Shirley Bassey

Shirley Bassey No.2

Shirley No.3

1962 Let's Face the Music

Shirley's Most Requested Songs

Till and Other Great Songs

1963 The Hits of Shirley Bassey

In Other Words...

1964 I (Who Have Nothing)

The Dynamic Shirley Bassey

Original soundtrack recordings

Year Song Movie

1964 "Goldfinger" Goldfinger

1965 "The Liquidator" The Liquidator

"The Liquidator" (alternative version)

"My Liquidator"

1968 "My Love has Two Faces" Deadfall

1971 "Diamonds are Forever"Diamonds are Forever

"Una Cascata di Diamanti" (Italian release only)

1979 "Moonraker" Moonraker

"Moonraker" (End Title)

1996 "'Disco' La Passione" La Passione

"Shirley, Do You Own a Ferrari?" (duet with Chris Rea)

2012 "Guardian of the Highlands" Sir Billi

Dame **Joan** Henrietta **Collins**, DBE, who was born on 23rd May 1933, in Paddington, London, England, UK then grew up during the Second World War, in Maida Vale in that city, is an actress, author and columnist. After making her stage debut in the Henrik Ibsen play A Doll's House, when aged 9, she trained as an actress at the Royal Academy of Dramatic Art (RADA) in London. She then signed an exclusive contract with the Rank Organisation, appearing in many British films.

Collins headed to Hollywood in 1955 when aged 22, having landed sultry roles in several popular films, including The Girl in the Red Velvet Swing (1955) and Rally Round the Flag, Boys! (1958). She continued to make films in the US and the UK throughout the 1960s, also guest-starring in an episode of the original Star Trek in 1967, "The City on the Edge of Forever", as Edith Keeler.

Her career went into decline during the 1970s, when she appeared in a number of horror films. Towards the end of the decade, Joan starred in two softcore pornographic films, based on best-selling novels by her younger sister Jackie Collins: The Stud (1978), followed by its sequel The Bitch (1979).

Joan then began appearing on stage, playing the title role in the British revival of The Last of Mrs. Cheyney in 1980, before a decade later having had a lead role in the revival of Noël Coward's Private Lives. Collins was given the role of Alexis Colby during 1981, the vengeful and scheming ex-wife of John Forsythe's character, in the 1980s soap opera Dynasty, winning a Golden Globe Award for Best Actress in 1982. She's credited with having played a big part in the success of Dynasty, which was the most-watched TV series in the US during the 1984-85 broadcast season. Joan received a star on the Hollywood Walk of Fame in 1983.

Collins was made a Dame by Queen Elizabeth II for services to charity, in 2015. Since the late 1970s, Joan has written several books, including some on beauty and autobiographies, having published her first novel, Prime Time, during 1988. A member of the Conservative Party, Collins was invited to attend the funeral of former Prime Minister Margaret Thatcher, during April 2013.

Joan was the daughter of Elsa Collins (née Bessant), a dance teacher and nightclub hostess, and Joseph William Collins (died 1988), an agent whose clients included Shirley Bassey, the Beatles, and Tom Jones. Her father, a native of South Africa, was Jewish, while her British mother was Anglican.

Joan had two younger siblings, Jackie (1937–2015), a novelist, and Bill, a property agent. She was educated at the Francis Holland School, an independent day school for girls in London, before training at the Royal Academy of Dramatic Art. When aged 17, Collins was signed to the J. Arthur Rank Film Company, a British film studio.

Collins made her feature debut as a beauty contest entrant, in Lady Godiva Rides Again (1951), which was followed by The Woman's Angle (1952), in a minor role as a Greek maid then the more significant role of a gangster's moll, in Judgment Deferred (1952). Joan's big break came when the Rank Organisation signed her for a major role, in I Believe in You (1952).

Her roles during the following year included Cosh Boy, in which she received 2nd billing, directed by Lewis Gilbert; Decameron

Nights; Turn the Key Softly; and The Square Ring, also having been loaned out to appear in Our Girl Friday, in which Collins was top of the bill. Gilbert used her again in The Good Die Young (1954), in which she starred with Laurence Harvey.

Joan was chosen by director Howard Hawks to star in his lavish Hollywood production of Land of the Pharaohs (1955), as the scheming Princess Nellifer, opposite Jack Hawkins. The film was a box office disappointment but Collins' performance led to a contract with 20th Century Fox, which gave her the role of Elizabeth Raleigh in The Virgin Queen (1955), in support of Richard Todd and Bette Davis.

She then played the title role in The Girl in the Red Velvet Swing (1955) as Evelyn Nesbit, which had been intended for Marilyn Monroe. The following year MGM borrowed her for The Opposite Sex (1956), a musical remake of The Women (1939), with Collins in a part originally played by Joan Crawford. Back at 20th Century Fox she played a nun in Sea Wife (1957), having also been one of several stars that year in The Wayward Bus, followed by Island in the Sun.

Collins starred as the female lead in Stopover Tokyo (1958), playing opposite Robert Wagner then The Bravados (1958), with Gregory Peck. She was a temptress for Paul Newman in the comedy Rally Round the Flag, Boys (1959), before completing her contract at 20th Century Fox with the crime caper Seven Thieves (1960), followed by the biblical epic Esther and the King (1960). Joan then starred in The Road to Hong Kong (1962), the last "road" picture of Bing Crosby and Bob Hope, having replaced Dorothy Lamour as the female lead, who Crosby had deemed to have grown too old.

Collins then took a break from movies to concentrate on having a family, after marrying Anthony Newley, before resuming her career, concentrating mainly on American TV. Her guest appearances on TV during the 1960s and 1970s included those in Batman, The Virginian, Mission: Impossible, Police Woman, and the original Star Trek, playing the role of Edith Keeler in the episode "The City on the Edge of Forever". Joan also made a guest appearance alongside Roger Moore and Tony Curtis, on ITV's series The Persuaders! as Sidonie, in the episode from 1972, 'Five Miles to Midnight'.

Collins also made movies in the 60s, including Hard Time for Princes (1965) in Italy; Warning Shot (1967), a drama; Subterfuge (1968), a thriller; and If It's Tuesday, This Must Be Belgium (1969), a comedy; She also appeared in Anthony Newley's autobiographical, Can Heironymus Merkin Ever Forget Mercy Humppe and Find True Happiness? (1969). At the start of the new decade Joan starred in a thriller with George Peppard, The Executioner (1970), followed by a quasi sequel to Three in the Attic, Up in the Cellar (1970).

During the early 1970s Collins returned to the UK, starring in a series of British films, mostly thrillers and horror movies: Revenge (1971), a thriller; Quest for Love (1971), a romantic science fiction piece; Tales from the Crypt (1972), an anthology horror; Fear in the Night (1972) psychological horror from Jimmy Sangster; Dark Places (1973), a horror; and Tales That Witness Madness (1973), another horror anthology. Joan then travelled to Italy for L'arbitro (1974), before returning to the UK for the horror I Don't Want to Be Born (1975).

Collins starred in some sex comedies in the mid-70s, Alfie Darling (1975) and The Bawdy Adventures of Tom Jones (1976), before returning to the US to make the sci-fi epic Empire of the Ants (1977). Joan then travelled to Italy again for Fearless in 1978, followed by The Big Sleep then a small role in Zero to Sixty, in England.

That same year Collins starred in the film version of her sister Jackie Collins's racy novel The Stud, which was a box office hit made for $600,000, grossing over $20,000,000 internationally. During 1979, after starring in Game for Vultures and Sunburn, she appeared in a sequel to The Stud, The Bitch, which was another hit, leading to Joan being offered a major role in US TV in 1981.

Collins was given the role of Alexis Carrington in the 2nd season of the then-struggling new soap opera Dynasty (1981–89), the beautiful and vengeful ex-wife of tycoon Blake Carrington, played by John Forsythe. Her performance is generally regarded as having been a big factor in the fledgling show's meteoric rise in the Nielsen ratings, to become a hit rivaling Dallas. While starring in the show, Joan also appeared in Homework and Nutcracker during 1982.

Dynasty was the # 1 show in the United States during 1985, ahead of Dallas, at # 2. Collins was nominated 6 times for a Golden Globe Award for her portrayal of Alexis, during every year from 1982 to 1987, winning in 1983, Joan thanking Sophia Loren for turning down the part of Alexis in her acceptance speech. That same year she was nominated for an Emmy as Best Actress in a Drama Series then at the age of 50, Collins appeared in a 12-page photo spread for Playboy magazine, shot by George Hurrell.

Joan also starred in Making of a Male Model in 1983, with young model-actor Jon-Erik Hexum, before in 1984, she played a soap star in The Cartier Affair, with David Hasselhoff and co-hosted the ABC-TV special Blondes vs. Brunettes. With Dynasty at the height of its success, Collins began producing, having starred in the 1986 CBS miniseries, Sins, followed by Monte Carlo, the first having had good ratings, but the 2nd being a critical and ratings flop.

In the 2001 E! True Hollywood Story episode featuring Dynasty, former ABC executive Ted Harbert stated, "The truth is we didn't really believe that we had this thing done as a hit until Joan Collins walked down that courtroom aisle." Co-star Al Corley observed that Collins "just flew" in the role that was "tailor made...just spot on." In Dynasty producer Aaron Spelling's final press interview, he said of Joan: "We didn't write Joan Collins. She played Joan Collins. Am I right? We wrote a character, but the character could have been played by 50 people and 49 of them would have failed. She made it work."

Collins took time off after the end of Dynasty in 1989, before rejoining her co-stars for Dynasty: The Reunion, a 1991 miniseries that concluded the series, which had been left with a cliffhanger ending following its abrupt cancellation. Joan made several guest-star appearances during the 1990s, on series including Roseanne, The Nanny and Will & Grace. She also appeared as the main characters of movies including Decadence (1994) and Annie: A Royal Adventure! (1995), in the latter of which she played the main antagonist, Lady Edwina Hogbottom.

Collins played Amanda, during 1990, in a revival of Noël Coward's Private Lives, later appearing in the same play in 1992, starring alongside Simon Jones. Joan also appeared in Noël Coward's Tonight at 8:30 during 1991 then was chosen as the cover model for the relaunch of the celebrity magazine OK! when it changed from being a monthly to a weekly.

Collins was cast in the film version of musical theatre show Joseph and the Amazing Technicolor Dreamcoat (1999), having played 2 roles in the movie, a pianist and the wife of Egyptian millionaire Potiphar. The following year Joan joined the cast of The Flintstones in Viva Rock Vegas (2000), a prequel to the Universal Studios live-action film The Flintstones (1994).

Collins reprised the supporting role of Pearl Slaghoople, Wilma Flintstone's mother, that Elizabeth Taylor had previously played. In 2001, she co-starred in the TV film These Old Broads with Debbie Reynolds, Shirley MacLaine, and Elizabeth Taylor, in her final role. The movie was written for TV by Debbie Reynolds's daughter, Carrie Fisher.

Joan returned to soap operas the following year, with a limited guest run on the American daytime soap, Guiding Light. Alice Krige impersonated Collins in Dynasty: The Making of a Guilty Pleasure in 2005, a fictionalised TV film, based on the creation and behind-the-scenes production of Dynasty. She also joined the cast of the hit British TV series Footballer's Wives for a limited run.

Joan toured the UK early the following year, in An Evening with Joan Collins, a one-woman show in which she covered the highs and lows of her career and life, which was directed by her then husband, Percy Gibson. She then reunited with her Dynasty co-stars for the nonfiction special Dynasty Reunion: Catfights and Caviar, later that year having begun a tour of North America, in the play Legends! with former Dynasty co-star Linda Evans, which concluded in May 2007, following a 30-week run.

Joan also guest-starred in the BBC series Hotel Babylon in 2006, as a lonely aristocrat desperate for romance. Collins appeared in "They Do It with Mirrors," a 2-hour episode of the murder-mystery drama Marple in 2009, as Ruth Van Rydock, a friend of detective Miss Jane Marple.

It was announced on 24th January 2010 that Collins was joining the German soap opera Verbotene Liebe (Forbidden Love) for a short run. She played an aristocratic British woman, Lady Joan, who took a young prince, played by German actor Stephan Kaefer, in tow. Collins started shooting on 22nd February 2010 then appeared on-screen during April 2010, also having served as a judge on Miss Ukraine Universe that year.

Joan made her pantomime debut in Dick Whittington as Queen Rat, at the Birmingham Hippodrome, during the 2010 Christmas season, starring alongside Nigel Havers, Keith Harris and Julian Clary. In May 2013, Collins announced on her Twitter profile that she'd be joining the cast of the British sitcom Benidorm in a guest role. That year she had a voice role in the animated feature film Saving Santa then starred in the fantasy Molly Moon and the Incredible Book of Hypnotism, which was slated for release in 2015.

People magazine reported that Joan would guest-star on the forthcoming E! drama series The Royals during August 2014, as the Grand Duchess of Oxford, the mother of fictional British Queen Helena, played by Elizabeth Hurley. Collins backed the children's fairytales app GivingTales in aid of UNICEF, during June 2015, together with other stars including Roger Moore, Ewan McGregor, Stephen Fry, Joanna Lumley and Michael Caine.

Ryan Murphy announced that Joan had joined the cast of American Horror Story during April 2018, for its upcoming 8th season, which she later confirmed herself in an Instagram post. No further details were revealed about the role, except that she would play the grandmother to Evan Peters' character, Collins having described the part as "glamorous."

Joan has been married 5 times, first to Northern Irish actor Maxwell Reed, whom she wed on 24th May 1952, after he allegedly raped her, getting divorced in 1956, before having an affair with actor Harry Belafonte during the filming of Island in the Sun, during 1957. Collins met 22-year-old actor Warren Beatty in 1959, to whom she became engaged during the early 1960s, but his infidelity led to their split.

Joan revealed in her 1978 autobiography that she became pregnant by Beatty but had an abortion. She then married actor and singer-songwriter Anthony Newley in 1963, followed by American businessman and manager Ron Kass in 1972, having had 2 children, Tara and Sacha, with Newley then a third, Katyana, with Kass.

Her marriage to Kass ended in divorce in 1983 then on 3rd November 1985, Collins married Swedish singer Peter Holm in a ceremony in Las Vegas but they were divorced on 25 August 1987. Joan married her 5th husband, Percy Gibson (born 1965), on 17th February 2002, at Claridge's Hotel in London. By 2013, Collins had 3 grandchildren.

Joan has homes in London, Los Angeles, New York City, and France, having described her life in 2010 as being "that of a gypsy". Her younger sister was Jackie Collins, a romantic novelist, who died in September 2015, Joan having been told only 2 weeks before her sister's death of the breast cancer she'd had for over 6 years.

Collins joined the UK Independence Party on 24th May 2004, after decades of dabbling with British politics. However, during early 2005, Joan commented that she'd rejoined the Conservative Party, stating, "The Labour Party doesn't care about the British people." Since the late 1990s Collins has been a guest diarist at The Spectator, also having written occasionally for the Daily Mail, The Times, The Daily Telegraph and The Lady in the UK, and Harper's Bazaar in the US.

Joan signed on to the Sunday Telegraph during September 2008, as a weekly opinions columnist for the final quarter of the year, before leaving to pursue other projects. She was a supporter of the late prime minister Margaret Thatcher, having been invited to attend Thatcher's funeral on 17th April 2013. Collins has also stated "I'm a big monarchist and I love the Queen," having supported British withdrawal from the European Union.

Joan has supported several charities for decades, while sponsoring several foster children in India for over 25 years. Collins spoke before the U.S. Congress in 1982, in support of increasing funding for neurological research. The following year she was named a patron of the International Foundation for Children with Learning Disabilities, having been awarded the foundation's highest honour in 1988, for her continuing support. The Joan Collins Wing of the Children's Hospital of Michigan in Detroit also opened that year, before in 1990, she was made an honorary founding member of the National Society for the Prevention of Cruelty to Children.

Joan was awarded the lifetime achievement award from the Association of Breast Cancer Studies in Great Britain in 1994, for her contribution to breast cancer awareness in the UK. Collins is patron of Fight for Sight and in 2003, she became a patron of the Shooting Star Chase Children's Hospice in Great Britain. Joan serves her former school, the Royal Academy of Dramatic Art, as the Honorary President of the RADA Associates.

Collins is a successful author of the bestselling novels, 'Prime Time', 'Love & Desire & Hate', 'Infamous' (aka 'Too Damn Famous'), 'Star Quality', 'Misfortune's Daughters' and 'The St. Tropez Lonely Hearts Club'. She's also written 6 lifestyle books, 'The Joan Collins Beauty Book', 'Health, Youth & Happiness: My Secrets', 'My Friends' Secrets', 'Joan's Way: Looking Good, Feeling Great' (aka 'The Art of Living Well'), and 'The World According to Joan', as well as memoirs, 'Past Imperfect', 'Katy: A Fight for Life', 'Second Act' and 'Passion For Life'. She's sold over 50 million copies of her books which have been translated into 30 languages.

Collins was embroiled in a high-profile legal battle with the publisher Random House, during the 1990s, which was televised daily on Court TV. Joan had signed a 2-book deal with the company for $4 million, which had given her a $1.2 million advance. Collins delivered a 690-page manuscript of a novel to

Random House during September 1991, entitled The Ruling Passion.

However, the publishing firm deemed the manuscript to be of such poor quality that they demanded the return of the $1.2 million advance they'd paid to Collins, stating that she'd failed to deliver completed books as per her contract. Joan countersued, arguing that her contract only required her to submit a "complete manuscript," not an "acceptable" one. As she'd provided 2 novels to the publishing company, A Ruling Passion in 1991 then a 2nd novel, Hell Hath No Fury, in 1992, as her contract stipulated, she argued that Random House owed her the remainder of the $4 million, also having contended that Random House hadn't provided the editorial assistance she'd expected.

Her Random House contract, negotiated by agent Irving Lazar, required that she be paid even if her completed manuscripts weren't published. When the case was finally heard in February 1996, a court determined that Collins could keep the advance given to her, plus a further $1 million for the first completed manuscript, but that the publisher didn't have to pay for the 2nd manuscript, as it was essentially a reworking of the first. Guiness World Records stated that Joan held the record for the world's largest unreturned payment for an unpublished manuscript.

Memoirs

Past Imperfect: An Autobiography (1978)

Katy: A Fight for Life, A Memoir (1982)

Second Act: An Autobiography (1996)

Passion For Life: An Autobiography (2013)

Nonfiction

The Joan Collins Beauty Book (1980)

Portraits of a Star (1987)

My Secrets (1994)

Health, Youth and Happiness: My Secrets (1995)

My Friends' Secrets (1999)

Joan's Way: Looking Good, Feeling Great (2002)

The Art of Living Well: Looking Good, Feeling Great (2007)

The World According to Joan (2011)

Fiction

Prime Time, a novel (1988)

Love and Desire and Hate, a novel (1990)

Too Damn Famous, a novel (1995), retitled Infamous for US (1996)

Star Quality, a novel (2002)

Misfortune's Daughters, a novel (2004)

The St. Tropez Lonely Hearts Club, a novel (2015)

By other authors

Joan Collins by John Kercher, Gallery Books (1984)

Joan Collins, Superstar: A Biography by Robert Levine, Dell Publishing (1985)

A Touch of Collins by Joe Collins, Columbus Books (1986)

Inside Joan Collins: A Biography by Jay David, Carroll & Graf Publishers, Inc. (1988)

Hollywood Sisters: Jackie and Joan Collins by Susan Crimp and Patricia Burstein, St. Martin's Press (1989)

Joan Collins: The Biography of an Icon by Graham Lord, Orion (2007)

TV ads

Collins appeared as a teenager in a Gas Board Commercial during the early 1950s.

In the early 1970s, she appeared in TB and magazine ads for British Airways, in which she was referred to as their "Most Frequent Flyer of First Class", a title she's maintained, having promoted the airline for more than three decades.

In 1978, she appeared alongside Leonard Rossiter in a series of Cinzano TV commercials, in which the drink was spilled down her dress. It was named as one of the Top 100 British Adverts in a Channel 4 poll.

In the mid-1980s, Joan appeared in print ads for Canada Dry Ginger Ale and Sanyo, and was the face of Revlon's Scoundrel perfume. In 1992, she appeared in internationally broadcast TV commercials for Marca Bravaria beer, while acting as the face of the perfume Spectacular.

Since 2000, she's appeared in TV ads for UK retailer Marks & Spencer, Olympus cameras, and Old Navy. In 2007, Collins fronted 2 high-profile ad campaigns, the first having been as the face of skincare company Cellex-C's Ageless 15 Skin Serum, the 2nd was acting as the face of the Royal Mail's Christmas campaign.

In 2010, Joan was named as the face of Alexis Bittar Jewelry for Spring Fashion Week then in 2012, she appeared in an ad for Snickers chocolate bars, alongside Stephanie Beacham, although the ad was later re-edited, with Beacham's appearance being cut.

Collins has sung publicly on many occasions, having performed "It's Great Not To Be Nominated" at the Academy Awards in 1959, with actresses Angela Lansbury and Dana Wynter. In 1962, she sang "Let's Not Be" in the film The Road to Hong Kong with Bing Crosby and Bob Hope.

Joan teamed up with Peter Sellers and her then-husband Anthony Newley in 1963, to record the album Fool Britannia, which made the UK Top 10. In 1968, she sang a zodiac-themed duet with Newley, titled "Chalk & Cheese", in Can Hieronymus Merkin Ever Forget Mercy Humppe and Find True Happiness?

Collins's role in the 1986 mini-series Monte Carlo was as Katrina Petrovna, a singer who doubled as a spy; "The Last Time I Saw Paris" was one of the songs she sang in character. In 2001, Joan sang several songs in the TV movie These Old Broads, including Get Happy, having appeared in Badly Drawn Boy's video for "Spitting In The Wind" that same year.

Honours

Collins was appointed Officer of the Order of the British Empire (OBE) in the 1997 New Year Honours for services to drama then Dame Commander of the Order of the British Empire (DBE), in the 2015 New Year Honours, for services to charity.

Awards

1957: Star of Tomorrow

1957: Motion Picture Magazine Award, Most Promising New Star

1978: Saturn Award nomination, Best Actress in a Science Fiction film, Empire of the Ants

1982: Golden Globe nomination, Best Actress in a TV Series (Drama), Dynasty

1982: Hollywood Women's Press Club, Female Star of 1982

1983: The Hollywood International Spotlight Award

1983: Golden Globe, Best Actress in a TV Series (Drama), Dynasty

1983: Star on the Hollywood Walk of Fame, Career Achievement

1984: People's Choice Award, Favorite female television performer, Dynasty

1984: Soap Opera Digest Award, Outstanding Villainess in a Primetime Drama Series, Dynasty

1985: Soap Opera Digest Award, Outstanding Villainess in a Primetime Drama Series, Dynasty

1986: Soap Opera Digest Award nomination, Outstanding Villainess in a Primetime Drama Series and Outstanding Actress in a Comic Relief Role in a Primetime Drama Series, Dynasty

1986: Telegatto Television Awards, Best Actress in a TV Series (Drama), Dynasty

1996: OBE (Officer of the Order of the British Empire) bestowed by H.M. Queen Elizabeth II for her contribution to the arts and ongoing charity work

1999: Millennium Award of Achievement, Golden Camera Film Council

2005: Lifetime Achievement Award, San Diego International Film Festival

2010: New York City International Film Festival, Best Actress, Fetish

2010: Beverly Hills Film, TV and New Media Festival, Best Actress, Fetish

2013: Lifetime Achievement Award, Sedona International Film Festival

2014: Awards "Freedom of the City of London"

2015: DBE (Dame Commander of the Order of the British Empire) for services to charity (in the 2015 New Years Honours List)

2016: Arts for India, Lifetime Achievement Award

2017: The Global Gift Philanthropist Award

2018: Pacific Pioneer Broadcasters Art Gilmore Career Achievement Award to Joan Collins

Filmography

Film

Year Title Role Notes

1951 Facts and Fancies short film

1951 Lady Godiva Rides Again Beauty Queen Contestant uncredited

1952 The Woman's Angle Marina

1952 Judgment Deferred Lil Carter

1952 I Believe in You Norma Hart

1953 Decameron Nights Pampinea / Maria

1953 Cosh Boy Rene Collins

1953 Turn the Key Softly Stella Jarvis

1953 The Square Ring Frankie

1953 Our Girl Friday Sadie Patch

1954 The Good Die Young Mary Halsey / Mary

1955 Land of the Pharaohs Princess Nellifer

1955 The Virgin Queen Beth Throckmorton

1955 The Girl in the Red Velvet Swing Evelyn Nesbit Thaw

1956 The Opposite Sex Crystal

1957 Sea Wife Sea Wife

1957 The Wayward Bus Alice Chicoy

1957 Island in the Sun Jocelyn Fleury

1957 Stopover Tokyo Tina Llewellyn

1958 The Bravados Josefa Velarde

1958 Rally 'Round the Flag, Boys! Angela Hoffa

1960 Seven Thieves Melanie

1960 Esther and the King Esther

1962 The Road to Hong Kong Diane

1964 Hard Time for Princes Jane

1967 Warning Shot Joanie Valens

1968 Subterfuge Anne Langley

1969 Can Heironymus Merkin Ever Forget Mercy Humppe and Find True Happiness? Polyester Poontang

1969 If It's Tuesday, This Must Be Belgium Girl on Sidewalk cameo appearance

1969 L'amore breve Roberta

1970 The Executioner Sarah Booth

1970 Up in the Cellar Pat Camber

1971 Revenge Carol Radford

1971 Quest for Love Ottilie / Tracy Fletcher

1972 Tales from the Crypt Joanne Clayton Segment: "And All Through The House"

1972 Fear in the Night Molly Carmichael

1973 Dark Places Sarah Mandeville

1973 Tales That Witness Madness Bella Thompson Segment: "Mel"

1974 L'arbitro Elena Sperani

1975 I Don't Want to Be Born Lucy Carlesi

1975 Il richiamo del lupo Sonia Kendall

1976 Alfie Darling Fay

1976 The Bawdy Adventures of Tom Jones Black Bess

1976 Il pomicione

1977 Empire of the Ants Marilyn Fryser

1978 Fearless Brigitte

1978 The Big Sleep Agnes Lozelle

1978 Zero to Sixty Gloria Martine

1978 The Stud Fontaine Khaled

1979 Game for Vultures Nicolle

1979 Sunburn Nera

1979 The Bitch Fontaine Khaled

1982 Homework Diane

1983 Nutcracker Laura Carrere

1994 Decadence Helen / Sybil

1995 In the Bleak Midwinter Margaretta D'Arcy

1996 The Line King: The Al Hirschfeld Story herself

1997 Coronation Street: Viva Las Vegas! herself

1999 Joseph and the Amazing Technicolor Dreamcoat Mrs. Potiphar

1999 The Clandestine Marriage Mrs. HeidelbergAlso associate producer

2000 The Flintstones in Viva Rock Vegas Pearl Slaghoople

2004 Ellis in Glamourland Susan

2006 Ozzie Max Happy

2007 Le Cirque: A Table in Heaven herself

2008 Valentino: The Last Emperor herself

2010 Fetish Francesca Vonn short film

2013 Saving Santa Vera Baddington voice

2014 Molly Moon and the Incredible Book of Hypnotism Nockman's Mother

2016 Absolutely Fabulous: The Movie Joan Collins

2017 The Time of Their Lives Helen Shelly Also executive producer

Television Year Title Role Notes

1964 The Human Jungle Liz Kross Episode: "Struggle for a Mind"

1966 Run for Your Life Gilian Wales Episode: "The Borders of Barbarism"

1966 The Man from U.N.C.L.E. Baroness Bibi De Chasseur / Rosy Shlagenheimer Episode: "The Galatea Affair"

1967 The Virginian Lorna Marie Marshall Episode: "The Lady from Wichita"

1967 Batman The Siren (Lorelei Circe) Episodes: "Ring Around the Riddler" and "The Wail of the Siren"

1967 The Danny Thomas Hour Myra Episode: "The Demon Under the Bed"

1967 Star Trek Edith Keeler Episode: "The City on the Edge of Forever"

1969 Mission: Impossible Nicole Vedette Episode: "Nicole"

1972 The Persuaders! Sidonie Episode: "Five Miles to Midnight"

1972 The Man Who Came to Dinner Lorraine Sheldon TV Movie

1973 Drive Hard, Drive Fast Carole Bradley TV Movie

1973 Great MysteriesJane Blake Episode: "The Dinner Party"

1974 Fallen Angels Jane Banbury TV pilot

1975 Ellery Queen Lady Daisy Frawley Episode: "The Adventure of Auld Lang Syne"

1975 Switch Jackie Simon Episode: "Stung from Beyond"

1975 Space: 1999 Kara Episode: "Mission of the Darians"

1976 Baretta Lynn Stiles Episode: "Pay or Die"

1976 Police Woman Lorelei Frank / Prudence Clark Episodes: "The Pawn Shop" and "The Trick Book"

1976 Arthur Hailey's the Moneychangers Avril Devereaux TV Mini-Series

1976 Gibbsville Andrea Episode: "Andrea"

1977 The Fantastic Journey Queen Halyana Episode: "Turnabout"

1977 Future Cop Eve Di Falco Episode: "The Kansas City Kid"

1977 Starsky and Hutch Janice Episode: "Starsky and Hutch on Playboy Island"

1979 Tales of the Unexpected Lady Natalia Turton Episode: "Neck"

1980 Tales of the Unexpected Clare Duckworth/Julia Roach Episode: "Georgy Porgy"

1980 Tales of the Unexpected Suzy Starr Episode "A Girl Can't Always Have Everything"

1980 Fantasy Island Lucy Atwell Episode: "My Fair Pharaoh/The Power"

1981–1989 DynastyAlexis Morell Carrington Colby Dexter Rowan series regular (Season 2-8), recurring (Season 9) 195 episodes

1982 Tattletales Herself TV Game Show

1982 Paper Dolls Racine TV Movie

1982 The Wild Women of Chastity Gulch Annie McCulloch TV Movie

1983 The Love Boat Janine Adams Episode: "The Captain's Crush/Out of My Hair/Off-Course Romance"

1983 Making of a Male Model Kay Dillon TV Movie

1983 Hansel and Gretel Stepmother / Witch TV Movie

1984 Her Life as a Man Pam Dugan TV Movie

1984 The Cartier Affair Cartier Rand / Marilyn Hallifax TV Movie

1986 Sins Helene Junot TV Mini-Series, also executive producer

1986 Monte Carlo Katrina Petrovna TV Movie, also executive producer

1991 Red Peppers Lily Pepper TV Movie, also executive producer

1991 Tonight at 8.30 Various Series regular, 8 episodes, also executive producer

1991 Dynasty: The Reunion Alexis Morrell Carrington Colby Dexter Rowan TV Movie

1993 Roseanne Ronnie Episode: "First Cousin, Twice Removed"

1993 Mama's Back Tamara Hamilton TV pilot

1993 Egoli: Place of Gold Catherine Sinclair Special Guest Star

1995 Annie: A Royal Adventure! Lady Edwina Hogbottom TV Movie

1995 Hart to Hart: Two Harts in 3/4 Time Lady Camilla TV Movie

1996 The Nanny Joan Sheffield Episode: "Me and Mrs. Joan"

1997 Pacific Palisades Christina Hobson 7 episodes

1998 Sweet Deception Arianna TV Movie

2000 Will & Grace Helena Barnes Episode: "My Best Friend's Tush"

2001 These Old Broads Addie Holden TV Movie

2002 Guiding Light Alexandra 'Alex' Spaulding von Halkein Thorpe Special guest star

2005 Slavery and the Making of America Reenactor Episode: "Seeds of Destruction"

2006 Hotel Babylon Lady Imogen Patton Episode: "1.7"

2006 Footballers' Wives Eva De Wolffe Episodes: "5.5" and "5.6"

2009 Agatha Christie Marple: They Do It with Mirrors Ruth Van Rydock TV Movie

2010 Rules of Engagement Bunny Dunbar Episode: "Les-bro"

2012–2013 Happily Divorced herself 3 episodes

2014–2017 Benidorm Crystal Hennessy-Vass recurring

2015–2018 The Royals Alexandra, Grand Duchess of Oxford recurring

2018 American Horror Story TBA Season 8

Theatre

1946, A Doll's House, at the Arts Theatre, London.

1952, The Seventh Veil, at the Q Theatre, London.

1952, Jassey, at the Q Theatre, London.

1953, The Praying Mantis, UK Tour.

1953, Claudia and David, at the Q Theatre, London.

1954, The Skin of Our Teeth, at the Q Theatre, London.

1979, Murder in Mind, at the Yvonne Arnaud and Theatre Royal, Guildford & Brighton.

1980, The Last of Mrs. Cheyney, at the Chichester Festival Theatre, Chichester.

1981, The Last of Mrs. Cheyney, at the Cambridge Theatre, London.

1990–1991, Private Lives, at the Aldwych Theatre, London.

1991–1992, Private Lives, at the Broadhurst Theatre, New York City.

2000, Love Letters, US Tour.

2001, Over the Moon, at the Old Vic Theatre, London.

2004, Full Circle, UK Tour.

2006, An Evening with Joan Collins, UK Tour.

2006–2007, Legends, North American Tour.

2010, One Night with Joan, at Feinsteins at the Regency, New York.

2010–2011, Dick Whittington, at the Birmingham Hippodrome, UK

2011, One Night with Joan, Australian Tour.

2011–2014, One Night with Joan, at the Leicester Square Theatre, London.

2012, One Night with Joan, at the Alban Arena, St Alban's, Hertfordshire, UK.

2012, Joan Collins: One Night in the Hay, at the Theatre Royal Haymarket, London.

2012, One Night with Joan, at the De La Mar Theatre, Amsterdam, Netherlands.

2013, One Night with Joan, UK Tour.

2016, Unscripted, UK Tour.

2017, One Night with Joan, Dubai operahouse in Dubai.

Lightning Source UK Ltd.
Milton Keynes UK
UKHW011842170119
335726UK00009B/333/P

9 781388 000745